BE THE
HERO
OF YOUR OWN
LIFE STORY

BE THE
HERO
OF YOUR OWN
LIFE STORY

SHANE BARKER

BOOKCRAFT
Salt Lake City, Utah

Library of Congress Catalog Card Number: 94-70491
ISBN 0-88494-922-2

First Printing, 1994

Printed in the United States of America

For Steve

CONTENTS

Contents

KARL MALONE AND EINSTEIN-THINK-ALIKES

Be the Hero of Your Own Life Story

K arl Malone!"

Jeff Whiting exploded from his seat, spilling his drink and dropping a whole bag of popcorn. "Look," he said. "It's *Karl Malone!*"

I swept a pile of popcorn off my lap and looked. Sure enough, Karl Malone—the star of the Utah Jazz—was coming down the aisle. Six feet nine inches tall, he was impossible to miss. He towered over the droves of people piling into Cougar Stadium.

Jeff couldn't take his eyes off him. An energetic ninth-grader who lived for basketball, Jeff was the world's biggest Jazz fan. His bedroom was covered with Jazz posters, programs, basketballs, and autographs. He never went out in public without wearing a Jazz hat, Jazz shirt, Jazz socks, Jazz *something*.

He was such a Jazz fanatic I was sure that if he 'cut himself he'd bleed purple.

Down on the football field, BYU was about to play Miami, the number one team in the nation. But Jeff wasn't even watching: Karl Malone was coming!

And then—Jeff's eyes nearly popped—the Mailman sat down . . . just two rows in front of us.

Jeff's eyes were as big as dinner plates. "Wow!" he said. "He's going to sit right there! I'm going to get his autograph!"

Before I could stop him, Jeff had bolted from his seat. He bounded down the steps and handed the Mailman his program.

"Could I have your autograph? Please?"

I'm sure Karl wasn't thrilled to spend the ballgame signing autographs, but with a happy grin he signed his name across the top of Jeff's program.

Jeff was beside himself! He practically floated back to his seat. He didn't take his eyes off his hero during the whole game, and when Karl left during the fourth quarter, Jeff noticed the score for the first time.

"Hey," he said, drawing stares from everyone around us. "We're winning!"

Now, you probably have heroes too. You might like a famous athlete, for instance; or a popular musician or movie star. Maybe you even admire someone your own age. Someone who's attractive, talented, or successful.

Whoever it is, wouldn't it be fun being in that person's place? Wouldn't it be great having people admire *you?* Wouldn't it be fun knowing that people plastered *your* picture all over their bedroom walls?

It could happen, you know. Really! Because you don't have to have the body of a beauty queen for people to admire you. You don't have to be a superman with rippling muscles to become a hero.

Let me give you an example.

I used to coach a Little League baseball team. One morning we were playing the best team in the league. We were in the middle of a losing streak, and we weren't just expected to lose. We were expected to get killed.

But we played our hearts out, and by the last inning we were behind by a single run. With two outs, we had runners on second and third. All we needed was a base hit to win the game.

The only problem was that Steve McClaren was up to bat.

Now, Steve was one of my favorite players. He was a good right fielder and he had a sense of humor that kept everyone happy—even when we were down by a dozen runs or so. But he was the worst hitter on the team.

I tried to be optimistic as he dug himself into the batter's box. "C'mon, Steve," I shouted. "Base hit wins the game, bud! Be a hitter, now!"

Steve took a couple of practice swings, then leaned over the plate.

"You can do it, Steve!" I shouted. "Give it a ride, now! Smack it out of here!"

Steve stared toward the pitcher. The ball came in high and tight . . . a tough pitch to hit.

Steve swung anyway.

And smacked the ball past the shortstop!

He bolted for first as both base runners charged home. The umpire held his mask in the air.

We'd won the game!

The team exploded from the dugout, swarming onto the field and piling on Steve like they'd just won the World Series.

I couldn't believe it. We'd won! We'd beaten the best team in the league! I was so choked up I couldn't move.

And Steve!

We had good athletes on the team. But Steve was the last person on earth I would have picked to win the game for us.

But like I said, *anyone* can be a hero.

Even you!

You might never sink the winning shot in a basketball game. You might never rescue a little kid from a burning house. And you might never star in your own music video. But you can be a hero in the life of the most important person in the world. You!

Consider this diagram:

Lazy Larry   0   Perfect Paul
                                    |
_____

On one end we have Perfect Paul. He's everyone's idea of a hero, because he succeeds at everything he does. Not only is he the starting quarterback on the football team but he's also the student body president and the class valedictorian; and he dates a cheerleader.

You probably know somebody just like him.

On the other end is Lazy Larry. You probably know somebody like him, too. His only hobby is watching TV, though he sometimes takes a little time out for video games, snacks, and comic books.

Now, chances are you're somewhere in between. And if you're like most people, you measure your success in life by how close you are to Perfect Paul. The closer you are, the better you feel. And the further away you are, the worse you feel.

But that's not right. Why? Because real success is not determined by where you are on the line. The only thing that matters is *which direction you're going.*

You could be clear down next to Lazy Larry. But as long as you're *doing the best you can* to move up the line, you're doing just fine.

4

And that's how you become the hero of your own life story. By keeping yourself moving up the line. By reaching difficult goals. Doing things you thought you were too scared to try. Reaching new heights. Pushing yourself to your fullest potential.

You do it by daring to be your very best self.

I teach school. When I handed back tests to one of my pre-algebra classes one day, a young woman named Kari took her test, looked it over, and jumped straight in the air. "Yes!" she shouted. "Yesyesyesyesyes . . ."

Everyone in the room turned to look, and it wasn't long before someone asked to see her test. Kari displayed it proudly. Everyone was expecting to see "100%" written at the top, and they were surprised to see that she'd only received an 85.

"What are you so excited about?" someone asked.

Kari pointed to her test. "I got number fifteen right."

"Number fifteen" was an exercise that combined a rectangle, a triangle, and a couple of half circles into one long, nightmarish problem. (It was the sort of thing that made you understand why they call them "problems.")

Kari had struggled with the concept all year, and she had worked and sweated and studied trying to get the hang of it. This was the first time she'd ever got the answer right on a test.

My class included several Einstein-think-alikes, and most of them couldn't understand what all the fuss was about. But I did. I had seen the effort Kari put into her study. I knew how hard math problems were for her. And in my mind she was more successful that day than students who yawned, scratched, stretched, and still managed to get 95 or 100 percent.

Sure, they were farther down the line than Kari, but they weren't going anywhere.

Remember that being your own hero doesn't mean you have to get straight A's on every report card. It doesn't mean being able to slam-dunk a basketball or becoming the world's first teenage brain surgeon.

It's quietly, consistently doing the best you can. It's realizing where you are on the number line and then honestly trying to do better.

A schoolteacher named Hal has been one of my heroes for a long time. We worked together at Boy Scout camp and often had long talks after work.

One time, late at night, we were sitting outside the camp lodge talking when he shared his personal secret for success.

"I made a two-year plan," he told me. "I decided that for two years I would do one new thing every day to make myself a better person."

That idea struck me like a lightning bolt, and I immediately tried it myself. Since I was working at Scout camp at the time, I did one new thing every day to make myself a better leader.

I couldn't believe what happened. I became more focused, more energetic, more fun-loving than ever before. Every day became an adventure as I created new programs and events. I made dozens of new friends and had the time of my life.

It was the most exciting, satisfying summer of my life.

A few years later I became a schoolteacher. It was fun, but after a couple of years I noticed my classes becoming dull and stale.

So I applied Hal's plan again. Every day I did one new thing to make myself a better teacher.

The difference was incredible! Teaching was suddenly more than just another job. It was an adventure! I went to work every day feeling excited and energized, anxious to get started.

Even my students noticed the difference. Two or three times a day, someone would ask, "How come you're in such a good mood?"

The answer was easy. I was having fun! Every day—every *class*—was an adventure.

Try it yourself.

If you're still in school (and you probably are), do one new thing every day to make yourself a better student. The first day you might commit to keeping notes in each of your classes. The next day you could resolve to keep your folders organized. One day you might promise to improve your handwriting.

This may not seem like a big deal, but if you begin on the first day of school, by the end of the year you'll have 180 things going for you.

And the exciting thing is that this plan will do more than help you in school. You can apply it to music; sports; relationships; testimonies. Even missionary work.

Think about it. If you simply improve by one percent—just *one* percent—every day, imagine where you'll be a year from now.

How can you *not* succeed with a plan like that?

Go back to the number line and take a good, long look at it. Try to decide *exactly* where you fit in. And don't cheat by putting yourself right in the middle. Commit yourself to one side or the other.

Now ask yourself as honestly as you can, *which direction am I going?*

As long as you're moving up the line, you're doing great! This book will show you how to keep it up.

And if you're not moving—or if you're not moving very fast—then this book is *really* for you. It will show you how to fill your life with excitement and energy.

Because you *can* be a hero. You can energize other people. You can bring out the best in your family and friends. You can spark your own life, finding more fun, success, and excitement than you ever knew possible.

So do it! Start now!

Be the hero of your own life story!

How to Get Started

- Decide to be the hero of your own life story. Don't just say it's something you *could* do. And don't just say it's something you *should* do. Decide that it's something you absolutely *will* do!

- Begin keeping a journal. Besides writing the details of your life, use it to record your goals and measure your progress.

- Pick an aspect of your life that's important to you. (Something like school, music, art, or sports.) Resolve to do one new thing every day to make yourself better at it. Write these things down in your journal.

- Take another look at the number line. Remind yourself that success isn't determined by where you are, but by *which direction you're going!* Commit to keeping yourself moving up the line.

2

HOW TO GET
A REBOUND

Energizing Your Life with Goals

C oach Ericksen was drawing on the gym floor with a piece of chalk.

"You've got to force them into the trap," he said, tapping his chalk. "If you can do that, they'll make bad passes. They'll make mistakes. Okay? Then let's do it."

The team huddled up, shouted "Win!" and jogged onto the floor.

An assistant coach, I took my seat on the bench and reached for my clipboard. I was nibbling the tip of my pencil when Scott Blackwell bounded over.

"Fifteen," he said.

I looked up. "What?"

Scott tapped my stat sheet. "Fifteen," he repeated. "Rebounds. I'm going to get fifteen rebounds tonight. I want you to write it down."

I laughed. "What are you talking about?"

"My dad made a bet with me," he explained. "He said he'd take me to a Jazz game if I could get fifteen rebounds tonight."

"Okay," I said, making a note in the margin. "Fifteen rebounds. Go for it!"

I grinned as Scott trotted away. Fourteen years old, he was a good athlete, but he lacked steam on the court. Fifteen rebounds! On his best night he'd never pulled down more than eight.

But suddenly Scott was a player with a purpose. He played like a wild man. Anytime anyone took a shot he crashed the boards, fighting for the ball. He played like Michael Jordan, bolting around the court, flying through the air, jumping more aggressively than he ever had in his life.

I couldn't believe the difference.

Scott got his fifteen rebounds, all right. And he scored a game-high eighteen points, too. Once he caught a glimpse of his own potential he became unbeatable.

That's the magic of goals. They fill your life with purpose and direction. They bring out your best self. They help you turn dreams into reality.

Now, I know you've heard all about goals before. And you probably think they're as exciting as soggy corn flakes and three-day-old oatmeal.

But don't stop reading! I'm going to show you how goals can energize your life. How they can do more than simply help you get things done, how they can fill your life with high-voltage excitement.

When I was in high school I had a friend named Rhett who was a good example. When he was twelve, he sat down and listed seventy-nine things he wanted to do by the time he was sixteen. He wanted to ride in a hot-air balloon, for instance. He wanted to sink a three-point shot in the Marriott Center. He wanted to become an Eagle Scout.

Some of his goals were spiritual, like receiving his patriarchal blessing, reading the Book of Mormon, and memorizing all the missionary scriptures.

Other goals were educational. He wanted to read *Moby Dick,* for instance. He wanted to win a spelling bee, take calculus, and make the honor roll.

And some of his goals were just plain off-the-wall. He wanted to make his own fishing pole, find a dinosaur bone, and learn to play the guitar.

Do you think his goals energized his life?

You bet they did!

One weekend he'd be out cross-country skiing, and the next he'd be flying an F-16 simulator at Hill Air Force Base. He was *always* doing something incredible. His life was filled with more adventures than most people his age even dream about.

Goals can do the same thing for you. They can put you on a collision course with success. They can shoot you down the number line at breakneck speed.

The key is following through. Most people have trouble doing this because their goals are no fun. It gets so they actually *dread* even thinking about them. It's no wonder they never accomplish anything!

So what you have to do is be creative. You have to ask yourself, how can I reach this goal and have fun while I'm doing it?

I remember a time when I decided to start an exercise program. I had an exercise bike, and I resolved to ride it for half an hour every day.

But it was no fun! I found that thirty minutes on a stationary bike is worse than an hour at the dentist. It got so I was searching for excuses not to follow through.

So I changed plans. I have a neighbor who loves

basketball, and we made a deal. We went out and played for half an hour every day after school. It was great! Suddenly exercise was something I looked forward to. And I got a lot better workout playing ball than I ever did on my bike.

You need to do the same thing: Find ways to make your goals fun. Make them exciting! Make them so much fun that you look forward to working on them.

Marcia, a young woman I know, decided she was going to become first-chair clarinet in her high school band. To help her do that, she resolved to practice for an hour every day.

Now, if you play an instrument, you know how boring that can be. But Marcia was creative. She called a bunch of friends together, organized a Dixieland band, and played with them for an hour every day before school.

Instead of being dull and tedious, practice was suddenly fun! Not only did Marcia become first chair but also her little band earned a hundred dollars playing at a Mardi Gras dance.

Like I said, goals can energize your life. But they'll never work unless you do. So here's how to get yourself started.

Begin by asking yourself, what's something that I really want to accomplish? What is it that I'd really like to do?

As you think about this, let yourself dream. Let your imagination run wild. Be *crazy!* What sort of things would you go for if you absolutely knew that you wouldn't fail?

Take flying lessons, for instance?
Try out for the school play?
Be first violin?
Pass your math class?
Learn to scuba dive?
Get a date to the prom?

Make the honor roll?
Learn to ski?
Learn to clog?
Buy a car?
Read the Book of Mormon?
Gain a testimony?
Get a job?
Write a story for the *New Era?*

There are no limits here. Write down *anything that you really feel you'd like to do.*

Have you done that?

Good. Now look over your list and pick out two things . . . two things that would fill you with excitement. Things that would really make you feel great about yourself.

Got 'em?

Okay.

Now comes a key step. Write those goals down as specifically as you can. Don't simply write that you want to be a better trombone player, for instance, or a faster runner.

Instead, be specific. Describe *exactly* what you want to achieve. For instance, you write something like this: "I am going to be first-chair trombone by the end of the month. And I am going to stay first chair for the rest of the year." Or, "I am going to break 5:00 in the mile run this year." Or, "I am going to get an A in biology this term. And I'm going to make the honor roll."

Again, be specific. The more clearly you understand what you want to accomplish, the more power you'll have to do it.

Next, carefully consider each goal. Then next to each one, list two or three things you could do *right now* to begin to achieve it.

Next to your music goal, you might write: "I will practice for forty-five minutes every day. I will practice my scales until I can play each of them *perfectly* in less than thirty seconds."

Next to your track goal, you might write: "I will run five miles every day before school. I will listen to my coach and eat only the kind of food that will keep me healthy."

Next to your school goal, you might write: "I will do all of my homework before I watch TV or take off with my friends. I will ask my teachers for help when I need it. I will spend twenty minutes every day working on my research paper."

As you do this, remember to find ways to make your goals fun! Instead of something you dread—something you do because you *have* to—make your goals something you look forward to!

Now comes the most important step of all. *Start working.* Don't waste another minute. If there's *anything* on your list that you could start on this instant, then *do it!*

Grab your trombone and start playing.
Get down to the track and run a couple of laps.
Get your homework done.
Start on that research paper.

I'll make you a promise. If you'll start now—if you'll take those things you listed and start on them *this minute*—you'll feel instantly better about yourself. And you'll have taken a critical step in becoming the hero of your own life story.

So do it! Start now and get momentum working for you.

Get going!
Now!

How to Get Started

- List two goals that you could really get excited about. Goals that would get your heart pumping. Goals that would really make you feel like a hero. Describe them as clearly as you can.

- Next to each goal, list two or three things you could do *right now* to begin to achieve them.

- Remember to ask yourself, how can I do this and have a great time doing it?

- Now get working. If there's anything you could do this instant, then *do it*. Get working! Get momentum on your side!

- Place your goals where you can see them every day. Keep them in mind! Keep yourself excited about them!

- Share your goals with your parents or other close friends. Seek their help and support in reaching them. Let them monitor your progress.

- Remember to seek your Heavenly Father's help. Not only can He give you the strength and courage to reach difficult goals but also He can give you help, inspiration, and direction along the way.

- As you begin to accomplish things, start over. Choose two or three new goals and get working on them, too.

3

THE "AHA" EXPERIENCE

Imitating Success

Brian Schultea waded knee-deep in the river and held out his fly rod. Whipping the line back and forth, he cast until his fly was *exactly* where he wanted it, then let the line settle on the water. A second later it went slicing through the current.

"Shane!" he shouted. "I've got another one!" He reeled furiously. "Wow! Look at him go!"

I couldn't believe it. "*Another* one? What do you do, Brian, use the Force?"

Brian just laughed. "Come on; give me a hand."

I put down my pole, grabbed the net, and waded into the river. A moment later an arc of silver flashed through the water. I waited until I saw it again, then plunged the net beneath the surface and pulled out a huge brown trout.

"Wow!" Brian said. "That's a *big* fish."

He gently removed his hook and lowered the fish back into the water. The trout remained still for a moment as it regained its bearings, then suddenly darted away.

Brian grinned.

I couldn't believe how good he was. In the hour we'd been fishing, he'd caught—and released—ten fish. *Ten!* It was amazing! I sometimes went for days without catching *one.*

But then, that's the reason we were fishing together.

Brian was a ninth grader in one of my geometry classes. He loved hunting and fishing, and he was good at it. He often came to class with stories of the dozen or so fish he'd managed to catch over the weekend.

"I don't know how you do it," I told him. "I fish the same holes you do. And I'm lucky to get a bite."

"It's no big deal," he told me. "You just have to use the right nymphs. And you have to use little tiny sinkers."

I knew there had to be more to it than that, so I went to see him in action. He gave me one of his "lucky" nymphs and showed me how he put his sinker about eighteen inches up the line.

It seemed too easy. But it worked. Just seconds after I started casting I had my first fish.

It was great!

I'd been fishing the Provo River for years. And every time I went out I got a little better. But in ten minutes of fishing with Brian I learned more than I had in ten years of trying it on my own.

Now, I'll bet there are things you'd like to be better at, too. Maybe you want to be a better musician. Or a better athlete. You might want to speak better French or be a more effective missionary. And as long as you work at those things, you're bound to improve.

But if you want to get better *fast,* there's a secret.

Find somebody who's good at it, and try it the way they do.

It's that simple.

I have a young friend named Heather who lives for dancing. Naturally athletic, she was born with more balance and coordination than most people ever have. Still, she says that her success comes from watching a dancer named Julie.

"Julie's the most incredible dancer I know," Heather said. "I could watch her for hours. She's been dancing since she was three, and she's in the *Nutcracker* every year at BYU."

But Heather does more than just admire Julie. She learns from her. She watches how she makes leaps and turns, skips and hops, jumps and kicks. Heather watches how Julie makes her entrances and how she plays to an audience.

Heather calls this the "Aha" experience.

"Sometimes I'll be working on a technique that just isn't coming," she said. "And then I'll see Julie do it and it's like, 'Aha! So that's how you do it!'"

And then she tries it the same way.

"I learn so much that way," Heather said. "I have good teachers, so I hate to say it, but I learn more watching Julie than I ever learn in class."

I know what she was talking about. I used to coach a boy named Scott on my eighth-grade basketball team. He was our best point guard, and besides being a good leader he was quick with his hands and fast on his feet.

"I wish I scored more points, though," he told me. "Like that kid who plays for Timpview. He's a guard, but he scores more than anyone else on the team."

I knew who he was talking about. Number Eleven. And Scott was right. He *did* score a lot of points.

So the next week Scott and I went to watch him play. And we learned something right away. Number Eleven wasn't a big kid, but he was smart. He'd bring the ball downcourt and drive for the key, forcing the defense to back up. But then—just before he reached the jam of people—he'd pull up, jump, and shoot.

It worked every time!

Scott was amazed. "I could do that," he said, suddenly excited. "I could really do that!"

And he did, too. He worked on it all week. Driving as hard as he could, he'd charge the key, abruptly stopping at the last second and launching the ball.

And the next game he gave it a try. The first time he got the ball, he attacked the key, suddenly pulling up, jumping, and shooting.

Swish!

The ball dropped through the net.

Scott pumped his fist through the air. "Yes!" he yelled.

The fun thing was that the play worked even better than he thought. As soon as the other team figured out what he was doing, they sent a player out to stop him. But that just opened up the key, allowing Scott to dish off to someone else.

Scott scored fourteen points that night. And it was all because of a trick he'd learned from watching someone else.

You can do the same thing. You come into contact with successful people every day. People who get good grades. People who are popular. People who are great musicians, great athletes, or great artists. Discovering what makes them so good can help you. Their secrets can be the guide to your success.

So if you want to be a great trombone player, find the best trombone player in your school and take a good look at him. Find out why he's as good as he is. Does he practice two hours a day? Take private lessons? Use a special mouthpiece?

Find out. And be specific. If he practices two hours a

day, find out what he works on. Fifteen minutes warming up? Ten minutes on scales? Fifteen minutes playing triads?

Find out. And then give it a try.

And if you want to be a faster runner, find the fastest runner in your school. Then discover why she's so good. Does she run ten miles a day? Eat or avoid certain foods? Swing her arms in a special way? Wear special shoes? Run sprints one day and distances the next?

It might be anything. Find out what it is, then give it a try.

After all, it worked for her. And it'll work for you.

I used to teach marksmanship at Boy Scout Camp. It was a fun class, but it was hard. To earn the Rifle Merit Badge, boys had to shoot five shots into a circle the size of a quarter. And they had to do it five times.

If you're a good shot, that might not seem like a big deal. But even our best rifles were old and battered. And many of them were so big and heavy that small boys had a tough time handling them.

But one week a boy named Walter signed up. Twelve years old, he was small and skinny and not very strong. Even so, he turned out to be the best shot in camp.

I couldn't believe how good he was. So I started watching him when he shot. Right away I noticed that he held his rifle differently than most boys. He positioned himself differently. He placed his hands and cheek on the rifle in ways I'd never seen before.

The same week there was another small boy in camp who was having a tough time. So I grabbed him and had him watch Walter.

"Look how he holds the rifle," I said. "And see how he puts his head on the stock? See if you can do it like that."

He did, and pretty soon he was shooting as well as Walter.

You can succeed in life by trial and error. You can try things over and over until you find something that works. But that's silly. Especially when there are successful people out there who can show you how to do it. Whatever good things you want to do in life—be a great missionary, a straight-A student, first-chair tuba—you're bound to know someone who can help.

And not only can these people show you what works; they can teach you what *doesn't* work, too. They can save you *hours* or *months* of wasted energy.

So take a minute to review the goals you listed in the previous chapter. Now, think of someone who's already mastered whatever it is you want to achieve.

If you want to be a great cheerleader, think of someone who's a great cheerleader. If you want to be a good student, think of the best student you know. And if you want to be a terrific dancer, think of someone who's a terrific dancer.

Now, figure out what they do that makes them so good. And don't be afraid to ask them! People love to talk about things they're good at. They'll be flattered that you're interested.

When I was in high school, my favorite hobby was archery. My best friend, Rick, was a national champion, and I wanted to be just like him.

One week I was practicing for a big tournament, and I knew that I needed to punch up my shooting if I wanted to win. So I called Rick.

"I need a favor," I said.

"Sure! What do you need?"

"I haven't been shooting so good lately," I said. "Is there any chance you could watch me? Maybe tell me what I'm doing wrong?"

"Sure," he said. "Let's do it."

An hour later he met me at the archery range, where he spent the rest of the afternoon giving me tips and pointers. That weekend I shot 35 points over my average, setting a state record.

And I won the tournament, too.

You can do the same thing. So if there's something in your life that you want to improve at, don't waste your time with trial and error. Find someone who's good at it and seek their help. Find out what their secrets are.

Then try them yourself.

You'll not only get better, you'll get better *fast!*

How to Get Started

- Consider the goals you listed in the last chapter. Now think of someone who's already mastered whatever it is you want to do.

- Next, find out why they're so good at what they do. Be specific. You never know what minor detail will unleash your own potential.

- Don't be shy. If you want to know the secret behind someone's success, don't be afraid to ask.

- Now give it a try. Remember that it worked for them, and it'll work for you.

AVOIDING THE ALL-NIGHT CRAM SESSION

Learning to Stay Ahead

The Mizlou play-by-play commentator was shouting into his microphone.

"Touchdown! *Unbelievable!* Brigham Young, in an absolutely unpredictable wild finish, has defeated SMU in one of the most spectacular college football endings I have *ever, ever* seen!"

I was on my hands and knees in front of the TV, not believing what I'd just seen. All around me people were jumping up and down, screaming, *hugging,* and slapping one another.

It was hard to believe what had just happened.

It was 1980, and BYU was playing Southern Methodist in the Holiday Bowl. Four minutes earlier, the Mustangs were whipping the Cougars 45-25.

There's not much a football team can do in four

minutes—especially when they're behind by twenty points—and people were leaving the stadium in droves.

But the Cougars weren't finished. Jim McMahon threw fifteen yards to Matt Braga in the end zone to make the score 45-31. BYU failed to make a two-point conversion but recovered an onside kick on the fifty-yard line.

The Cougars worked the ball down to the one-foot line, then ran around the right side for a touchdown. Seconds later Scott Phillips caught an 11-yard pass for two extra points.

With 1:58 left in the game, the score was suddenly 45-39.

Southern Methodist had the ball and tried to run out the clock. They ran four plays without going anywhere and had to punt.

BYU *blocked the punt!* With thirteen seconds left, the Cougars had the ball on the 47-yard line and a chance to win. McMahon threw twice into the end zone, missing his receivers both times. The clock stopped with three seconds left.

The Cougars had time for one last play. McMahon threw a bomb into the end zone. Clay Brown was there . . . and with no time left on the clock, BYU tied the score! Kurt Gunther booted the ball through the uprights to clinch the win.

BYU had beaten Southern Methodist 46-45.

It was one of the most spectacular comebacks in the history of college football.

In sports there's nothing as thrilling as making a come-from-behind win. You just can't beat the excitement of defying the odds to come from behind and go roaring ahead.

Even so, a come-from-behind win is *not* a wonderful strategy. It's not something you want to go out and do every game.

I used to help coach an eighth-grade basketball team. One night we were playing the best team in the league, and they were killing us.

But then, late in the game, we suddenly came to life. We started a full-court press, stealing the ball three times and scoring on the layups.

Scott Blackwell, meanwhile, our point guard, began playing like Michael Jordan, Scottie Pippin, and John Stockton all rolled into one. He sank three shots from three-point range, scored twice on layups, and went three-for-four from the foul line.

And suddenly, with seven seconds left, we were behind by a single point.

The coach called a timeout but didn't even outline a play. "You know how to break their press," he shouted over the noise of the crowd. "So do it. Make good passes. Then get the ball inside to Brian."

On the count of three everyone shouted "Win!" and took their places. Scott took the ball and passed it to Brian, our 6-2 center. Brian turned and lofted the ball toward the basket . . . and missed!

It was so close!

After playing our hearts out—coming so close that we had everyone in the crowd on their feet—we lost by a single point.

It was heartbreaking. We'd come so close to winning. As good as our effort had been, it was just a matter of too little too late.

As you get older you'll find that life is often like that. You *can* make the come-from-behind win. You might lose friends and still survive. You might fall behind in school, only to come roaring back and finish the term at the head of your class.

It can be done.

But if you want to succeed, the best strategy is to get ahead and stay ahead.

Let me give you an example.

I know a missionary who struggled with the lesson plan. He memorized and passed off each lesson to his senior companion, then promptly forgot it. So every time he taught a lesson, he had to spend the day brushing up on it. Sometimes—when they were having a good day— he had three or four lessons to learn. The next day he'd have three or four more.

Finally he came up with a better strategy. He got up one morning and spent the whole day memorizing the first lesson. He carried it with him all day, and as he pedaled from place to place he recited it in his mind.

The next day he did the same thing with the second lesson. He recited it again and again until he had it down cold.

The next day he worked on the third lesson. And by the end of the week, he knew the entire lesson plan. But this time he didn't forget it. Every morning—just before taking his shower—he sat down at his desk, closed his eyes, and recited a whole lesson—word for word—in his mind.

It took about twenty minutes. But he never again had to cram for a lesson. He was *always* prepared.

When you learn to stay ahead, many things actually become easier. Think about it. If you get behind in school, you have to spend a lot of extra time working, studying, and staying after school for help.

But when you make the effort to stay ahead, you eliminate those things. You still need to put time into your homework, but you avoid the extra time you need to catch up. You avoid having to stay after school to retake tests or get help from the teacher.

Try it! It works!

A couple of years ago I had a party at my home. And not being the world's tidiest person, I had a lot of cleaning to do to get ready. Every night for a week I spent time cleaning, washing, scraping, mopping, vacuuming, dusting, *burning,* organizing, and polishing.

What a pain!

I hated cleaning anyway. But to have so much to do was a real drag.

The worst part was my refrigerator. I found things growing fuzz in there that could have taken first place in any junior high school science fair.

Even now it gives me chills just thinking about it.

By the time I was done I hated housework, I hated my house, I hated all the people who were coming over and making me have to work so hard.

The whole experience was so painful that I changed tactics. I made a chart with all the rooms in my house listed on it. And now I take a few minutes to clean one room *every* day.

The nice thing is that now I never have to spend more than a few minutes cleaning. Besides that, the house is *always* clean. If I ever have company, I don't have to spend *any* time getting ready.

By keeping ahead of my chores, I actually have more time to spend doing things I *want* to be doing.

To be successful in life—to develop confidence and self-esteem—you have to do the same thing. You can't always be playing catch-up ball. You have to get ahead and stay there.

This principle applies to everything—missionary work, chores, even school.

A friend of mine named Marie was taking biology. The first several weeks of class were easy, so she didn't put a lot of time or effort into her work. She realized that if she just half-listened in class she could usually do well on her weekly tests.

As time went on, though, the material became tougher. But Marie didn't study any harder. She continued to half-listen in class and muddle her way through assignments.

You probably know what happened next. Marie fell behind. Worse than that, she came close to failing.

"My teacher mailed home a failing notice," Marie said. "And my parents flipped. They told me if I didn't get my grade up to a B, they were going to ground me for the rest of the term."

So Marie went to work. The only problem was that she was so far behind that she not only had to work on the new material but also had to catch up on all of the old work, too.

The sad thing is that Marie's mistake haunted her for the rest of the year. Missing out on a few basic concepts put her so far behind that she never did catch up completely.

You may have had similar experiences. If you have, you know how hard it is trying to catch up in a class once you've fallen behind.

So do your best to stay ahead!

If you want to succeed in school, stay current. Get working on your assignments as soon as you get them. Then, when the end of the term comes along, you'll be ready for it. You won't have to worry about trying to catch up.

If you want to succeed at your part-time job, do the same. Tackle assignments as soon as you get them.

Staying ahead in your work has another advantage. It gives you the luxury of tackling big projects a little at a time. You might have a big research paper to do, for instance. If you put it off, you guarantee yourself a miserable stay-up-till-midnight, skip-breakfast-lunch-and-dinner, get-an-ulcer cram session the day before the paper's due.

But if you start on it right away, you can divide the project into pieces. The first week you could spend twenty minutes a day researching. The next week you might begin sketching out your first draft. The third week you could start editing, polishing, and rewriting.

You might even have time for someone else to read your paper and offer suggestions.

A couple of years ago I proposed a book to a certain publisher. They liked my idea, but to fit the book into their schedule they had to have the final draft by the middle of February.

That wouldn't have been a problem, except that they didn't tell me that until the middle of December.

In other words, they gave me two months to write an entire book.

At first the project seemed overwhelming. But I knew I couldn't pass up the opportunity, so sitting down at my desk I devised a plan. Rather than worrying about the whole book, I took it page by page and chapter by chapter. That way it didn't seem so overwhelming. I was able to tackle the book in small, easy-to-handle chunks.

I actually finished the book in a month (being able to work over Christmas vacation helped), and was able to spend the last four weeks polishing, revising, editing, and trying to make it as good as possible.

When you get behind in the game of life, it frequently is possible to make the come-from-behind win. But the best strategy for success is to get ahead and stay ahead.

So learn to do things *now*. Tackle big projects a little at a time. Give yourself the luxury of doing things according to your own schedule.

Your life will not only become easier, it'll be a lot more fun, too!

How to Get Started

- Don't procrastinate. Learn to dive into your chores, homework, and work assignments as soon as you get them.

- If you constantly feel behind in something (like school) get working now to catch up. Get ahead. Then put in the effort to *stay ahead*.

- If your problem is just remembering to do things, buy a day planner.

- If you do get behind in something, *don't give up*. Fight back with all the strength and energy you have. Remember that you *can* make the come-from-behind win.

5

HOW TO GET A DATE

Overcoming Fears

Seventeen-year-old Sarah Lemke couldn't believe what she was about to do. Taking big, deep breaths, she tried to calm herself, then finally picked up the phone and punched in the number.

The phone rang once, twice, three times.

"Hello?"

Sarah's heart pounded. " 'ello"—her voice squeaked. She quickly cleared her throat. "Hello. Is this Aaron?"

"Yes, it is."

"Hi! My name is Sarah Lemke. You don't know me, but I'm Steve Marshall's next-door neighbor."

"Oh, hi."

"I know this is kind of sudden, but the girls in my ward are having a party Friday. We're going to make pizza and watch movies. My best friend is taking Steve, and since I know you guys are friends I was wondering if maybe you'd like to go with me."

Aaron laughed. "Well . . . yeah! Okay. It sounds fun!"

"All right!"

They made the final arrangements, and when Sarah hung up she was dizzy with excitement. Aaron was really going to go with her. It was incredible!

The funny thing was that it had taken her a week to gather enough courage to make the call.

"Aaron didn't even know me," she explained. "But I had seen him at school and was dying to meet him. I was terrified that he'd laugh or say no."

She was so worried, in fact, that she kept finding excuses not to call. She put it off for so long that she was on the verge of not doing it at all.

Then Steve stepped in.

"Aaron's great!" he said. "And he's not going to laugh at you. Call him!"

So, finally, Sarah did.

"And we had *so* much fun," she said. "I can't believe I almost didn't go through with it."

Have you ever had an experience like that? When you've been afraid to do or try something, only to find out there wasn't anything to be afraid of?

I have.

Fear is one of the biggest obstacles to becoming your own hero. It keeps you from trying things. It keeps you from venturing outside your "comfort" zone. It keeps you from realizing your potential.

It keeps you from discovering your best self.

I have a friend named Debbie who loves drama. And when her high school put on the play *Joseph and the Amazing Technicolor Dreamcoat*, she desperately wanted to audition.

But she was afraid to sign up.

"I knew I'd have to sing when I auditioned," she said.

"And I knew I'd have to do it in front of everyone else. There were lots of girls better than me trying out, and every time I saw their names on the sign-up list I'd chicken out."

At the last minute, though, she finally added her name to the sign-up list. She practiced reading, and—with her mother accompanying her on the piano—she prepared a song. She made callbacks, and second callbacks, and finally landed the part of the narrator.

"*Joseph* was the highlight of the whole year for me," she said. "It was *so* much fun! And I made so many friends!"

It boosted her confidence, too. She auditioned for every play that year, and the next year she joined the Shakespearian acting team.

I have another friend who wanted to try out for the football team. But he never did. And now—fifteen years later—he still wonders what he missed out on.

"It haunts me," he said. "Who knows? I might have been one of the best receivers in the state. And I still kick myself for not trying out. Whether I had made the team or not, at least I'd have known that I'd given it my best shot."

Don't let that happen to you.

Don't let fear keep you from trying new things. Don't let it keep you from asking people for dates, applying for jobs, or making new friends. Don't let it keep you from doing anything that would enrich your life.

When I was on my mission to Japan, we sometimes tried to make contacts on the street. We'd look for someone who didn't seem to be in a hurry, then casually approach and introduce ourselves.

It scared me to death.

I was just shy, for one thing. And I was afraid of making a mistake or being turned down.

I was so terrified, in fact, that whenever my companion

suggested "streeting" I'd feel cold knots wind up in my stomach.

But one day I changed my attitude. "I'm here to talk to people," I told myself. "And that's exactly what I'm going to do."

So I started talking to people right and left. And it was fun. I was nervous at first, but once I got the hang of it I really had a good time. It was just a matter of breaking the ice. Streeting went from being the low point of my mission to one of the highlights.

And the more fun I had, the better I got at doing it. There even came a time when my companion and I had so much success that other missionaries began calling to find out what our secret was.

It was great!

The neat thing is that most fears turn out just like that. You dread doing something so much that you put it off. But once you give it a try, it turns out to be not so bad. Sometimes it turns out to be fun. And then you end up kicking yourself for not doing it sooner.

Several years ago I decided that I needed a new job. I thought about it for a long time, but I never did anything because I was scared. The thoughts of marching up to someone I didn't know and asking for an application frightened me.

But finally I gathered my courage, put on my suit, and just did it. I was horribly scared, but that very fact made it an adventure. And it actually turned out to be fun.

The next time I went job junting I was just as scared. But I did something different this time. Instead of thinking about how scared I was, I kept reminding myself how much fun it had been the last time.

And it worked. Job hunting went from being terrifying to exciting.

When I was in high school I had a friend named Kurt who was absolutely fearless. If there was a girl he liked, he didn't waste time wondering if she'd go out with him. He'd pick up the phone and ask her.

When he decided to get a job, he didn't worry about being embarrassed or getting turned down. He scoured the mall, filling out application forms at every store that would give him one.

When we needed to borrow props from a local theater for a school assembly, he didn't hesitate. He drove straight to the theater and asked for them. And he got them!

I was at his home one time when he called and asked one of the school cheerleaders for a date.

"I don't know how you do it," I told him. "It'd scare me to death calling girls like that."

He looked surprised. "It scares me, too," he said. "But if it wasn't scary it wouldn't be fun."

If you want to be your very best self, don't let your fears stand in the way. Don't let them slow you down. Don't let them stop your progress. Don't let them stop you from doing things that would make you feel good about yourself.

The world is full of opportunities. To become your best self you have to take advantage of them. But if you're still afraid of doing or trying something, consider these tips.

First, *decide* that you're going to do it. This is important. You have to resolve that it's not just something you want to do. And it's not something you ought to do. Decide that it's something that you *absolutely will do!*

Make the decision, and then go for it with everything you've got.

Next, think of all the positive emotions you'll feel by doing it. If you've decided to apply for a new job, for instance, imagine how good you'll feel when you get it. Imagine being able to afford your own school clothes. Imagine being more independent, having your parents proud of you, learning responsibility, and making new friends.

List everything you can think of. Fill your mind with *positive* reasons to follow through.

Then list all the negative things you'll feel if you *don't* do it. You might feel like a quitter, for instance. You might end up with a crummy job when you could have had a good one. Your parents are going to be on your case.

Again, list everything you can think of.

As you do this, three things will happen. You'll feel a sense of urgency to get it done. You'll be less able to worry. And—if the emotions you listed are powerful enough—you might actually become afraid of *not* doing it. Which is a good point.

I've always been pretty shy, and when I was in high school the thought of calling a girl for a date was enough to give me the shakes.

But I had a friend named Nick who gave me a great bit of advice. "Don't be afraid of doing something like that," he said. "Be afraid of *not* doing it."

That thought has done more to end my fears than anything else. Whenever I get nervous about doing something, I just ask myself, "What will happen if I *don't* do it?"

Try it!

If you're afraid to apply for that job you want, remind yourself what will happen if you don't. (Picture yourself *never* getting a job . . . or imagine ending up with something worse.)

If you're afraid of trying out for the jazz band, think of what it will be like if you don't. (Picture yourself watching someone else playing in *your* spot for the rest of the year.)

If you're afraid to get a date for the prom, think of what will happen if you don't. (Won't it be fun sitting around and watching TV while someone else dances with the girl *you* like?)

Don't be afraid of doing things. Be afraid of *not* doing them.

If you really want to become your own hero, don't let fears stand in your way. Don't let them hold you back. Don't let them keep you from doing things that will enrich your life.

Don't waste another minute. Take the chance. Make the call. Ask for the date. Apply for the job. Try out for the team.

Do it now!

How to Get Started

- Think of something you've been putting off because you're afraid. Resolve that it's something that you are absolutely going to do. Decide to do it, and then go for it with *everything* you've got.

- If you need extra incentive, fill your mind with all the positive things you'll feel by following through. Write them down if you have to. Let these positive images crowd your fears out of your mind.

- Next, imagine all the negative things you'll feel by *not* following through. Make *not* doing it seem like the most horrible thing that could happen.

- Always remember this: Don't be afraid of doing things. Be afraid of *not* doing them.

6

SMILING IN THE RAIN

Taking Responsibility

David Shaw was as giddy as a little kid on Christmas morning. His eyes flashed with excitement and his grin covered his face.

"Okay," he said. "Here I go. Be right back."

He climbed out of the car and bounded across the lawn to the porch. He rang the doorbell, ran his fingers through his hair, and tried to look relaxed. A moment later the door opened and Dave went inside.

I couldn't help laughing. "Wow, is he in love or what?"

My date, Michelle, poked me playfully. "Are you that excited when you pick *me* up?"

I pretended to yawn and act nonchalant. "Well, no . . . "

She withered me with a you'd-*better*-be teasing expression, and I quickly added, "When I pick you up I'm a *lot* more excited than that!"

Michelle and I had been dating for several weeks, and we were doubling with Dave and his latest heartthrob. This was their first date, and Dave was so pumped up that he hadn't slept for the last two nights. Allison was not only a varsity songleader but also was one of the most popular girls in the school.

Dave was so intent on showing her a good time that he had the whole evening planned down to the finest detail. We were going to a Hawaiian restaurant for dinner. Then we were off to a laser show. Finally, we were going back to his house for hot-fudge sundaes.

As if that wasn't enough, he had spent the whole afternoon washing, waxing, polishing, and vacuuming his car.

It was going to be a great night.

After a couple of minutes, though, Allison's door opened and Dave came out . . . alone. He trudged across the lawn and climbed behind the wheel. He sat there for a minute, then turned to look at Michelle and me.

"She stood me up," he said quietly. "Some friends invited her to a party and she decided to go."

I wasn't sure what to say. I could feel the heartache in his voice. He sat for another moment, then looked again over his shoulder. He tried to sound cheerful.

"Well, hey . . . the night's young. You guys still game for a night on the town?"

We nodded. "Yeah. Sure."

"All right. Let's go get my sister. We'll have a great time."

And we did. Dave's sister Holly was nineteen—two years older than the rest of us—but she was great to be with. We had a blast.

Later, after we'd taken Michelle home and Holly had gone inside, Dave and I sat in his car and talked.

"Are you okay?" I asked.

He nodded. "Yeah, I'm fine. I was pretty disappointed,

but I'm okay now. I mean, I can't help what Allison does. So why should I let her ruin my life?"

At the time I didn't appreciate what he was saying. But I later realized that Dave knew the primary key to becoming his own hero.

He didn't let someone else's actions determine his happiness.

There's an important lesson there. You too have to take responsibility for your own success and happiness. You can't let someone else's actions, attitudes, or opinions do it for you.

I remember talking with a young woman who was failing her biology class. When I asked her why, she said, "Because I have the worst teacher in the world."

"And that's why you're failing?"

"Yes! He hates me."

"But why does that mean you have to fail?"

"Because he's so unfair!"

I just nodded. I'm a teacher myself, and I see students go through this all the time. (I hate to admit it, but sometimes *I'm* the teacher they're talking about!)

Angie's problem was that she refused to take responsibility for her own success. The fact that her teacher "hated" her made it okay for her not to take notes or complete assignments. The fact that he was a "bad teacher" made it all right not to listen in class or read her textbook.

In other words, it was *his* fault that she wasn't doing well.

The truth is, though, if Angie had really wanted to succeed she could have. She didn't have to let her teacher make the decision for her.

I have another friend named Seth who had a teacher like Angie's. One day Seth asked a question in class that made his teacher stop in his tracks.

"There's not supposed to be such a thing as a 'dumb'

question," Seth told me, "but I must have come pretty close. Mr. Rawlings put down his chalk, rubbed his eyes, and said, 'If you're still asking questions like that, you ought to be back in seventh grade.'"

Seth couldn't believe his teacher had said that! He felt so hurt that he didn't even want to go back to class.

But Seth decided that he wasn't going to let his teacher ruin his education. For the rest of the term he sat in the back of the room. He read his book carefully, going over key concepts until he understood them and completing each of his assignments.

He ended the term with a B, his highest grade of the year.

Seth understood what we're talking about here. He knew that having a nerd for a teacher was beside the point. *He* was still responsible for his own grade.

You need to learn the same thing. If you're having trouble in school, don't waste time blaming your teacher. That doesn't get you anywhere. Instead, do the best you can. Do everything *you* can to be a better student.

If you're having problems at home, don't blame your parents. That will only make things worse. Instead, do whatever *you* can to be a better son or daughter.

If you're not succeeding in sports, don't blame your coach. Go out and work and practice like there's no tomorrow. Do what *you* can to be a better player.

In each of these situations, things may not be exactly as you would like them to be. But few things in life ever are. And if life has to be perfect in order for you to be happy, you'll never make it.

So don't wait until you get a date to the prom. Don't wait until you make the team. Don't wait until your friends invite you over. Be happy now! Attack life with all the energy and enthusiasm you can. Make the best of what you have.

If you want to succeed in school, start now. Attack

your assignments with excitement and enthusiasm. Challenge your teachers to keep up with *you*.

If you want to succeed in sports, start now. Charge into every practice like you're being scouted for the pros.

Accept the fact that it's up to *you* to decide how happy or successful you're going to be. No one else can do it for you.

And don't let things that are beyond your control hold you back.

When I was thirteen, my Scout troop spent a week at summer camp. And it rained the whole time we were there. At first we were disappointed. As long as it was raining we couldn't go out on the lake (we might get hit by lightning). We couldn't shoot at the archery range (rain is hard on bows and arrows). And we couldn't go fishing (all the runoff made the lake too muddy).

Besides that, we couldn't swim in the pool, we couldn't shoot at the rifle range, and we couldn't study the stars.

It looked like we were in for a long, boring week.

But we had Scouts in our troop who didn't let the weather determine their happiness. So rather than spend the week moping in our tents, we put on our swimming suits and played Frisbee football in the meadow. We played steal the flag in the forest. One night we even hiked to a ridge called Frontiersman Flat, where we sat in our ponchos and watched the lightning storm as it lit up the valley.

The next day—as a service project—we volunteered to clean up the basement of the camp lodge. It was a real mess, and cleaning it turned out to be hard, dirty work. But we made a game of it and the camp—as a reward for our work—let us spend the afternoon shooting muzzle-loaders under the camp pavilion.

I know there were troops in camp that never left their tents that week. But we were determined to have a good time, and we weren't going to let anything as insignificant as a little rain stop us.

There will be times when rain, snow, or other conditions spoil your plans, too. But you can't let that dampen your spirit. After all, there's nothing you can do about changing such conditions. So instead of whining about the things you *can't* do, go out and look for things you *can* do.

This isn't always *easy* to do. When things don't work out right—or when someone close or important to you hurts your feelings—trying not to feel bad is something like walking into a storm and trying not to get wet. But if you have the determination, you can do it.

When I was in high school, our secretaries had an annoying way of calling for a custodian. They'd blare a sharp *BEEP* over the intercom. It was loud and irritating, and it always seemed to happen right when you were trying to concentrate on something.

One time, I was sitting in class studying for a test. The room was tense and quiet. Then suddenly, *BEEEEEP!*

It was so unexpected that everyone jumped.

"That is *so* annoying!" someone said.

"I agree," said Miss Lambert, our teacher. "So new rule. Anytime we hear that, everyone has to stand and we'll give ourselves a standing ovation. It'll be our signal to reward ourselves for being alive."

And so we did. The next time it happened, everyone jumped from their seats, cheering and clapping and feeling good.

It was a silly exercise. But it makes a point. You *can* become happy at the sound of a beep. You can become happy at the drop of a hat. You can become happy just by deciding to be!

So do it!

It takes a little effort. But you have the choice. You can let yourself be hurt by people and conditions you have no control over. Or you can decide that you're going to be happy—that you're going to do the very best you can—no matter what else happens.

So do it. Commit yourself to being a good student. Resolve to be a terrific athlete. Decide to be an incredible musician. Don't let the opinions or actions of others stand in your way. Set your own goals and then do your very best to reach them.

Most of all, be happy.

How to Get Started

- Don't let the opinions or actions of other people determine whether you'll be happy. Decide that you're going to be happy *no matter what.*

- Don't let other people determine your success. Even if they put up road blocks and stand in your way, continue to do the best that *you* can.

- Don't let rain, snow, or anything else beyond your control spoil your happiness. Make the best of whatever situation you're in.

- When things go wrong, don't waste time wondering *why* it happened. Instead, concentrate on solutions. Spend your time figuring out *what you're going to do about it.*

7

THE TEN-THIRTY
DOUGHNUT BREAK

Developing a Positive Attitude

Fifteen-year-old Jana Thomas stroked a paintbrush across a sheet of plywood. "I'm so tired," she said, patting away a yawn. "What time is it?"

I glanced at my watch. "It's ten-thirty."

"Is it A.M. or P.M.?"

"It's P.M."

She groaned. "That's what I was afraid of." She yawned again. "It feels more like midnight."

I just nodded.

The junior high school I taught at was going to present the play *Dracula*, and I was helping to build the set. Because we were behind schedule, this was the fourth school night in a row that we'd had to work late. Besides being tired, all of us were grumpy, moody, and irritable.

I was just dipping a brush in a can of paint—trying to

keep my eyes open—when the stage door flew open and Lisa Morgan burst through. She startled me so badly that I dropped my paintbrush.

"Doughnuts!" she shouted, holding up a large pink box. "I brought doughnuts for everybody! And cider, too!"

I took a moment to make sure my heart was still beating, then wiped up the spot of yellow paint on the floor.

"Come on," Lisa shouted again. "We're taking a ten-minute doughnut break. Last person here has to clean up."

She didn't have to ask again. We were all ready for a break. As we huddled around the snacks, Lisa popped a dance tape into a boom box and cranked up the volume.

The effect was magical. Minutes earlier we were all tired, short-tempered, and ready to quit. But moments after Lisa came bursting in we were excited, rejuvenated, and ready to get back to work.

You probably know people just like her. People who are always happy and energetic. People who bring out the best in you. People who make you feel good just by being around you.

The exciting thing is that *you* can be one of them.

I used to spend my summers working at Boy Scout camp, and I once took a group of Scouts on an overnight hike. It was a stormy, rainy day, and we had several miles to go—most of them uphill. I knew that within the first mile or two many of the boys would start grumbling. They'd complain about the hills, the weather, the mud, and everything else they could think of. They'd make the trip miserable for everyone.

So I took along a secret weapon . . . a boy named Kevin.

Kevin, sixteen years old, had the personality of a firecracker. He had an ear-to-ear grin and a zest for life that was positively contagious. He was a nonstop flurry of jokes, puns, and stories. From the minute we started out, Kevin had everyone feeling excited about the trip. He lighted a fire of enthusiasm that made the cold, rainy day an adventure.

There were boys on that trip who were natural moaners and groaners, but they never made a peep. They couldn't. They were having too much fun.

That's the power of a positive attitude.

Now, what about you? Are you generally positive about things? Are you optimistic? Happy? Upbeat?

Or are you negative, depressing, and pessimistic?

Whatever attitude you have, it's one that *you* choose. You have the power to maintain a happy outlook on life. You can charge the batteries and energize the lives of the people around you. That alone will make you stand out among your friends.

But it will make your own life more fun, too.

When I was on my mission, I had a companion named Elder Bonham. He was the most friendly, outgoing, optimistic, full-of-energy-and-ready-to-baptize elder I had ever known. Living with him was like living with a bottle rocket. Even on the hardest, most miserable days, his high-voltage personality kept things bright and cheery.

I admired him for that. And I wished that I could be just like him.

And then I realized that I *could* be. Elder Bonham didn't do anything that I couldn't do. After all, *I* could be happy. *I* could be optimistic. *I* could be energetic.

The moment I realized that, my mission changed. Every morning I got up trying to be as happy as I could. I tried to look for the bright side of things. I tried to be upbeat and optimistic.

It wasn't always easy. But the more I worked at it, the easier it became. And every night and morning, when I said my personal prayers, I asked for help in keeping it up.

And what a difference it made! I felt like a new person. I charged into my work with more energy than ever before.

You can do the same thing.

You may have seen the movie *Steel Magnolias*. My favorite line in it is the one where Ouiser says, "I'm not crazy . . . I've just been in a very bad mood for forty years."

How sad that would be! And yet some people approach life that very way. They focus on the bad in things rather than on the good. They spend all their time thinking about how sad or lonely they are. They worry about every little thing that goes wrong for them.

Don't do that!

In Sunday School and seminary you learn about the dangers of evil thoughts. But negative thoughts too are dangerous. They keep you from doing your best. They keep you from trying new things. They keep you from realizing your potential.

So wipe them out. Refuse to think them. Anytime a negative thought tries to surface, bury it beneath an avalanche of positive ones.

Remember that you can be just as happy as you choose to be.

You don't believe it? Then try this: Get up from where you're sitting and throw your shoulders back. Hold your head up. Take a deep, satisfying breath and laugh.

Are you doing it?

Good!

Now, march across the room. Don't just walk. *March.* Imagine how it would feel to be the most happy, confident, powerful person in the world, and stride in the way you think that person would.

Do it.

I know this sounds silly, but *doesn't it feel good* when you do that? Sure it does! And there's a simple reason for that. Your mind takes cues from your body. And marching around like the happiest person on earth triggers positive mental images in your mind. Your brain figures you must be happy. And then it's hard *not* to feel good.

Try it!

If you want to be more confident in school, don't slink in the door and slouch at your desk. Instead, stride to your classes as if you were the most successful person in the world. Sit up at your desk. Breathe deep. *Smile.*

And see if you don't feel better!

If you want to do better at work, in an audition, or in an interview, do the same thing. Throw your shoulders back and hold your head up. Smile. And *see* if you don't perform better. See if you don't have more fun.

Remember that attitude is a state of mind. And if you often feel sad or unhappy, it's simply because you let your mind dwell on the wrong things.

I remember a time when I was feeling down. Then the phone rang. It wasn't anyone important, but during the few minutes we talked I forgot how sad I was. My mind was busy thinking about something else.

And that's important. If you feel sad, lonely, or depressed, it's because you focus on sad, lonely, and depressing things.

So if you want to keep yourself feeling energized, start first thing in the morning. As soon as you wake up, give yourself exciting, vibrant images to focus on. You can do that by asking yourself questions like these:

—What's the most exciting thing I'm going to do today?

—Who's the most outrageous person I'm going to see?

—How can *I* make this the best, most enjoyable, most exciting day of my life?

Ask yourself each question. Really think about it. Then let your brain go to work. What *are* you excited about? A pep rally or assembly at school? A BYU football game? A special dance or Mutual activity?

And who *are* you excited to see? That cute boy in English? The girl who always smiles and says hi in the hall? A zany teacher who always makes the day more fun?

Let the images dance in your mind. Really focus on them. You'll hop out of bed *looking forward to the day*.

This might seem silly. But just try it. Do it every morning, then let these positive images energize you all day long.

And if you have trouble thinking of anything, *make something up*. Really! There was a time when my life seemed so gloomy that I had a hard time finding anything to be excited about. But I had a young neighbor who was a special friend. He'd done a lot of nice things for me, so I decided to do something in return. I decided to buy him a new baseball glove and give it to him secretly.

Suddenly I had something to look forward to. Something to be excited about.

You can do the same thing. And as you do you'll keep your mind focused on positive, uplifting things. Your life will become happier, more exciting.

Keep in mind that a positive attitude will not automatically make all your problems go away. But it *will* give you additional power to deal with them.

There's more to it than that, though. By working on a positive attitude you'll be happier and healthier. And when you cultivate a happy, upbeat attitude, you'll draw people like a magnet.

People *like* to be happy.

Having the right attitude will create a new person within you—a person everyone wants to know, enjoy, and be with. Including yourself.

Remember Ouiser. You can be in a bad mood for forty years, but why do that? Be happy. Be confident. Make each day a new adventure.

And you'll *be* the hero of your own life story.

How to Get Started

- Decide to be happy. Be optimistic. Be energetic. Resolve to be the firecracker who sparks life and energy in the lives of your friends.

- Refuse to think negative thoughts. Anytime one tries to surface, bury it beneath an avalanche of positive ones.

- Start every morning asking yourself these questions: What am I excited about? Who am I anxious to see? What am I most enthusiastic about? How can *I* make this the best day of my life? Get out of bed *looking forward to the day.*

- Remember that when you mope about, your brain thinks you must be depressed. So sit up straight. Open your eyes. Smile. *Train* yourself to be happy.

- Most important of all, don't just read these suggestions. *Try them.*

8

YOU'VE GOT YOUR
FEET ON THE BRAKES

Getting Rid of Baggage

W hen I was twelve I read a story in *Boy's Life* about two boys riding a bicycle-built-for-two. They were going uphill, and the boy in front was gasping for breath as he pedaled.

After huffing and puffing for several minutes, they finally reached the top and stopped for a rest.

"Wow!" the first boy said. "That was some hill. I didn't think we were going to make it."

"Neither did I," said his friend. "If I hadn't had my feet on the brakes, we probably would have rolled all the way down!"

It's a silly story, but it makes an important point. Sometimes we find ourselves pedaling as hard as we can to get somewhere, only to find that someone—or something—has the brakes on, holding us back.

Let me give you a couple of examples.

A friend of mine named Steve turns on the TV every day as soon as he gets home from school. "School gets me uptight," he told me. "So I like to just sit around to let myself relax and unwind." (I asked him once why he had to watch TV. He just shrugged and said, "What else are you doing to do with it?")

The only trouble is, TV is addicting. Steve only intends to watch for a few minutes. But you know how that goes. Once he starts watching, he *has* to see how the show ends. Then he waits just long enough to see what's on next. And the whole routine starts over again. He ends up watching two or three hours of TV every evening.

Meanwhile, he earns Cs and Bs in school because he never finds the time to get all his homework done.

I also have a friend named Corrine, who was taking a difficult biology class. She was usually a good student, but she sat near girls who were more interested in fashions, boys, and cheerleading than they were in biology. They spent their class time passing notes instead of taking them. They whispered back and forth when they should have been working. They discussed their plans for the weekend when they could have been helping one another understand the function of mitochondria.

While every one of them was capable of earning an A in the class, none of them received anything higher than a C.

Instead of helping one another to succeed, they were holding each other back.

Finally, I know a young woman named Kristin who wanted to audition for her high school's symphonic band. But she kept putting it off. When she was a sophomore she convinced herself that she was too young to try out. The next year she talked herself into believing that she wasn't good enough. It wasn't until her senior year, in fact, that she finally auditioned. (She was afraid of being the only senior in the lower band.)

The interesting thing is that she made it with no

difficulty. She quickly discovered that she was as good as anyone else in the band. She could have made it as a sophomore—and she probably could have been second or third chair, too.

The sad thing is that she let negative beliefs keep her from trying.

Now, there might be things in your life that hold you back, too. Like Steve, you might have habits that waste your time. Like Corrine, you might have friends who keep you from doing your best. Like Kristin, you might have negative beliefs that keep you from trying things.

The good news is that you can get rid of these things. The key is being aware of what they are and then taking action to eliminate them.

Are you willing to try?

Good!

Start by taking a piece of paper and dividing it into three columns. At the top of the first column, write the word *Habits*. At the top of the next one write *Friends*. And at the top of the last one write *Beliefs*.

Now that you've done that, under *Habits* list any habits that could be holding you back. Do you watch too much TV, for instance? Play too many computer games? Sleep in late? Procrastinate? Have a Word of Wisdom problem? Struggle with a moral problem?

Be honest with yourself and list anything you can think of.

Then do the same thing in the *Friends* column. Write the names of everyone who keeps you from doing your best. Everyone who's a bad influence. Everyone who makes you feel unimportant.

This is tough, I know. But relax. I'm not going to tell you to go and dump all of your best buddies. And no one is going to see your list but you. So go ahead—list everyone who could be holding you back.

Finally, consider your beliefs. Think you're not smart enough to get an A in math?

Write it down.

Think you're too ordinary to be friends with a cheerleader?

Write it down.

Worry that you're not good enough to audition for the school play?

Yup. Write it down. And list any other negative beliefs you have. You might not feel qualified to apply for a job, for instance. You might not feel good enough to try out for the team. You might not feel popular enough to ask for a date.

Again, list any belief or feeling that holds you back. Anything that limits you. Anything that makes you feel less than you really are.

Have you finished?

Okay. Now, take a deep breath and look at what you've written. Start with your habits. If you have habits that hold you back, break them. Replace them with habits that enhance and enrich your life.

Let's assume you watch too much TV, for example. In fact, take a minute and figure out how many hours of TV you watch every day. Two? Three? Four?

Four?

That's a lot of television!

So here's a challenge that I guarantee will change your life. Pick one of your best talents. Piano, for instance. Or writing. Or painting. Then, *for a whole week*, don't watch a minute of television. Instead, use the time developing that talent.

Try it.

Even if you only have to give up one hour of TV a day, you'll make incredible progress on your talent.

Remember that to be your best, you *have* to control your habits. You cannot let your habits control you.

Now consider your friends. Again, I'm not going to tell you to dump anyone. But consider the effect your friends have on you. If you spend time with people who pull you down—who keep you from being your best—you might as well be pedaling uphill and letting them hold the brakes.

So if you really want to be your best, be certain you spend time with people who bring out the best in you.

Finally, examine your beliefs. You might think you're too dumb to make the honor roll. You might think you're too ordinary to date a cheerleader. You might think you lack the talent to audition for the school play.

Baloney!

Who ever told you that you were dumb?

Huh?

And who told you that you were ordinary?

Chances are, no one's ever said those things to you. *You're* the one who planted those thoughts in your mind.

So stop it.

Instead of convincing yourself that you're dumb, ordinary, or untalented, program yourself to believe *positive* things.

You see, your brain is like a computer. It only acts on the information you feed it. If you constantly tell it you're plain or ordinary, it has no choice but to believe it.

Worse, it will *act* as if those things were true.

But if you constantly tell yourself you're smart, special, and talented, that's exactly what your brain will believe. In turn, your brain will react by giving you the power to *be* smart, special, and talented. ("As he thinketh in his heart, so is he," remember?)

So, beginning now, start reprogramming your brain. Fill it with positive, uplifting messages like these:

I *am* special.
I like who I am.
I feel good about myself.
I *am* smart.
I'm *full* of talent.

I have so much potential I can't stand it.
I *am* adventurous
(and I can't wait to see what I'll do next).
I have a *wonderful* personality.
I am outrageous.
My Heavenly Father *loves* me.

This may seem simple. But it works. And here's how you can prove it. Take a 3x5 card and write down four or five statements such as those listed above. Then, every day before you go to school, stand in front of the mirror, look yourself in the eye, and say them to yourself. Don't be wishy-washy, but say them like you really mean it. Say, "I *am* special! I *like* who I am! I'm *happy* to be alive!"

Then, do the same thing every night before you go to bed. Do it just as regularly as saying your prayers and brushing your teeth. As you do, you'll start to feel better about yourself. More than that, you'll start to *be* better.

Remember that you are *exactly* what you think you are.

Like an airplane with ice on its wings, everyone has things in his life that holds him back from time to time. Be aware of what they are. If you have unproductive habits, break them. If you have bad friends, replace them. If you have negative beliefs, change them.

Just see how much difference it makes.

How to Get Started

- Take a minute to evaluate yourself, and write down any habits that could be holding you back.

57

Take steps to rid them from your life. Start cultivating habits that will bless and enrich your life.

- Now consider your friends. Are they people who lift you up? Or do they hold you back? Make certain you spend your time with people who are motivating and supportive.

- Start programming your mind with positive, uplifting, empowering thoughts. Write down four or five statements like those listed earlier and repeat them to yourself every morning and night.

9

BURPING IN
THE MICROPHONE

Dealing with Mistakes

Callie Reardon took the basketball and held it over her head. "Go!" she shouted. She slapped the ball, sending her teammates criss-crossing over the court. In the confusion, Lindsey Turner managed to break free.

"Callie! *Callie!*"

Callie spotted her and lobbed the ball over the pack. Lindsey caught the pass perfectly and charged down-court. She could hear her coach and teammates scream-ing as she drove for the basket, laying the ball smoothly against the glass and into the net.

Two points!

Lindsey turned, expecting a flurry of high fives from her teammates. Only no one was cheering.

They were laughing.

It was several seconds before the awful realization set in.

It was the wrong basket!

Lindsey could have died. Instead of being the hero of the game, she was suddenly the laughingstock. The next day at school was even worse. No one mentioned the five steals she'd made; or the six foul shots. The only thing anyone talked about was her shot at the wrong basket.

"I had to live with people calling me 'Wrong-way Turner' for a month," she told me. "I didn't think they'd ever get over it."

I laughed, but I knew how she felt. I was riding my mountain bike once with my friend Mark. He was flying down the mountain like a kid fleeing Bigfoot, and I was struggling to keep up. I barreled over a rise and shot down the trail. Several teenage girls were standing at the bottom watching me.

I knew I should have slowed down, but I didn't want to look like a wimp. So I boomed down the trail at full speed. There was a bump in the trail halfway down, and when I hit it I lost control. I shot through the trees, smacking a log, and somersaulting through the air.

The fact that I wiped out made me feel dumb enough. The fact that I had an audience made me feel worse. But as I dusted myself off, one of the girls just *had* to rub it in.

"Hey," she said. "Your bike okay?"

I felt pretty silly, of course. But I'm sure you've had embarrassing moments, too. Everybody does. *Everybody!* It's a part of life, but that's not the point. It's how you *react* that counts. You can put your head in a hole and hope that everybody forgets. Or you can laugh at yourself and get on with your life.

I know a young woman named Karen who was supposed to sing a solo during her junior high school's Christmas concert. She was so nervous that she practiced for hours to make sure she'd perform perfectly.

Nothing she did, though, could possibly have prepared her for what happened. When the time to perform came, she stepped up to the microphone, opened her mouth . . . and burped.

She burped!

The entire audience roared with laughter.

At that moment, Karen faced a crucial decision. She could have run off the stage and never showed her face again. Or she could have gone on with her solo.

She decided to sing. As soon as the audience settled back down, she smiled and sang as best as she could.

"Singing that song was the hardest thing I've ever done," Karen said. "But I had to do it. I knew that if I didn't I'd only feel worse."

There's a good lesson there. When something embarrassing happens to you—and it will!—don't despair. Don't hide your head in a hole. It might feel like the world has come to an end, but the truth is that, in time, everybody forgets. So don't let it haunt you.

Laugh at it.

When I was in high school, I worked part-time at an ice-cream store. One night I was working by myself when a man asked for a hot-fudge shake.

"And could you make it with real hot fudge?" he asked.

"Sure," I said. "Why not?"

It wasn't the way we usually made shakes, but I didn't see any harm in making it the way he wanted. So I plopped a few scoops of vanilla ice cream into a cup, poured in a ladle of steaming hot fudge, then added a little milk. Then I placed the cup in the blender and flicked the switch.

Milk and ice cream exploded from the blender, spraying everything in sight.

I jabbed at the off switch, but it was too late. There was ice cream everywhere. It covered the walls and dripped from my face. I had to wipe my eyes just to see.

As soon as I regained my senses, I peered into the blender and saw what had happened. The hot fudge had reacted with the cold milk, hardening around the blender blades. Turning on the blender had been like turning on a jet propeller.

Everyone in the store was laughing. I wished I could have disappeared, but I was the only employee there and didn't have any choice but to make the best of a bad situation. So I simply took the near-empty cup, handed it to the customer, and said, "Would you like nuts on that, sir?"

I felt devastated when that "explosion" happened. (I hated getting laughed at!) But I can't even think of it now without laughing. Just the thought of my face covered with ice cream cracks me up.

You probably know what I'm talking about. No matter how embarrassing something is, it always seems funny later.

So why wait?

Laugh now.

It also helps if you don't think of your mishaps as mistakes. Think of them as lessons. Ask yourself, what can I learn from this?

When you concentrate on learning from your mistakes, it's easier to forget the humiliation. Besides, you can often learn a lot of good things from your mistakes.

I have a friend who played on his high school baseball team. He was playing centerfield when a batter cracked a fly right to him. It should have been an easy catch, but it popped out of his glove, making him look as uncoordinated as a little kid.

Instead of ending the inning, Justin let two runs score.

The nice thing is that his coach didn't get mad. When Justin trudged into the dugout a little later, his coach put an arm around him and said: "Okay. What did you learn out there?"

"To use both hands when I catch the ball."

"Are you going to remember that?"

Justin nodded. "Yes."

He did, too. He never again went for a fly ball without using both hands.

When you slip up, don't spend hours kicking yourself for your mistake. Instead, look at it as a learning experience. Learn from your mistake and move on with your life.

And don't let it get you down!

When something embarrassing happens, trying not to feel bad is like walking into a rainstorm and trying not to get wet. But sometimes you just have to make the best of a bad situation.

A friend of mine named Steve played drums in his high school's jazz band. He was good, and the band played a number that featured him in a shredding drum solo. Steve made a show of it, twirling his sticks, bobbing his head, and generally making a ham of himself.

Then, during a region competition, he was right in the middle of his solo when he lost one of his sticks. It went flying out of his hand and into the audience.

Everyone saw it happen. Everyone saw the stick go flying. Everyone knew Steve was in trouble.

But he didn't quit. He kept flaying away at his drums with his remaining stick for another thirty seconds, playing the best one-handed solo anyone there had ever heard. And when he finished, the audience gave him a standing ovation.

I remember a time my baseball team was playing our fiercest rivals. Our best pitcher, a boy named Clay, was on the mound. He had a sizzling fastball that could cook steaks. He had a wicked changeup, too. Holding the ball in the palm of his hand, he'd lean back, clench his face, and throw the ball with all the power he had, making the batter think he was throwing his fastball.

But since the ball was so far back in his hand, instead of streaking over the plate, it floated, fooling the batter into swinging too soon. Clay was so good that he could have struck out Henry Aaron with it.

Late in the game, when Clay was pitching against a kid who led the league in home runs, he decided to throw his changeup. He pulled back, clenched his face, and threw as hard as he could. But he was trying so hard that he lost his balance. The ball went straight in the air. Clay danced around, trying to regain his balance, then fell and landed flat on his back.

Everyone on both teams broke out laughing. Everyone in the stands was laughing. The umpires were laughing. Even I—as I ran out to see if he was okay—was laughing.

Even Clay was laughing.

I know he felt pretty dumb. But I'll never forget how he handled it. He stood up, dusted himself off, then bowed to the crowd.

Everyone cheered.

Then Clay took the ball and struck out the batter on three straight pitches.

When you slip up, it's easy to let the experience get you down. But there's no point in that. So don't worry about it. Forget it!

And remember that you're not the only one who makes mistakes. *Everyone* does.

A young woman I know played the part of Maria when her high school performed *The Sound of Music*. Even though she was just seventeen, Ana was an excellent actress.

Her only problem, in fact, was that she was just a little *too* good. She often contradicted the director and lectured other actors on how to play their parts. This made her look conceited and drew a lot of resentment.

But everything worked out on opening night. During the ballroom scene, she was making her grand entrance when she slipped on the floor. She landed flat on her rump with her dress flying up over her head.

Suddenly she wasn't Miss Hollywood anymore. She was human, just like everyone else.

You see, everyone makes mistakes. Sooner or later everyone gets his chance to be totally humiliated.

So when your turn comes, don't run off and hide your head in a hole. Learn from your mistakes. Laugh at yourself. Enjoy the experience.

That way, you'll avoid hours of misery. And your life will be more fun, too!

How to Get Started

- Think of something you've done that really embarrassed you. Instead of dwelling on how humiliating it was, think about how *funny* it was.

- Remember that, in time, even the most embarrassing things will seem funny. So don't wait. Laugh now.

- The next time you make a blooper, relax. Then see if there's anything you can learn from the experience.

- Don't let your mistakes get you down. Remember that *everybody* makes mistakes! Learn to forget them and move on with your life.

10

SCHUSSING ON THE ICE

Making Good Friends

Melissa Henry soared off the jump, kicking her heels up in a perfect backscratcher. She flew through the air, finally hitting the slope in a spray of powder. Unfortunately, she was going too fast, and her skis shot out from under her.

A shrill scream split the mountain air as she snowballed down the slope.

"Aaaaaaaiiiigh!"

Trying not to laugh, I skied down the slope, skidding to a stop and spraying her with snow.

"You okay?"

Melissa threw a snowball at me. She was covered with so much snow she looked like Frosty the Snowman. Her cheeks were flushed from the cold, but a smile covered her face.

"That was so much fun!" she said. "We have to do it again."

"Which part?" I asked. "The jump or the wipe out?"

She smacked me with another snowball, then picked herself up and skied to the crest of the next slope. "Let's race."

I nodded. "Okay . . . loser buys lunch?"

"You're on. On your mark, get set . . ." Without waiting for "Go!" she hit the slope. In a second she was schussing down the ice like an Olympic racer going for the gold.

"Cheat! Cheat!" I pushed off and folded into a tuck, trying to pick up speed. Melissa had a huge head start, but there was a wicked jump ahead and I knew I'd catch up when she skied around it.

I was feeling pretty smug about beating her when I heard a shriek and saw Melissa go flying off the jump. She sailed through space, hitting the slope in a puff of snow, and zipped on down the mountain.

I never had a chance.

"Hey," she said when I finally caught up with her. "Ready to buy lunch?"

Even though she was the world's biggest tease, I loved skiing with Melissa. She was so full of life and energy that when I was with her, I couldn't help but feel good myself.

Melissa and I worked together at an ice-cream store in the local mall. I was always glad when we were scheduled together, because she made work so much fun.

One time, for instance, I was busy scooping up ice cream for a banana split when she came up behind me and whispered in my ear.

"I bet I can make you laugh," she said.

"I bet you can't."

"We'll see!"

She danced away, greeting her next customer with her biggest Miss America smile. And then, with the most realistic southern accent I had ever heard, she blurted, "How y'all doin' tonight?"

I tried not to laugh, but I couldn't help myself.

She was *nuts*!

There were times when working at an ice-cream store wasn't the most exciting thing in the world. But when Melissa was around, it was *always* fun.

I loved Melissa for that. She was like my own personal cheerleader. Having her for a friend was like having a battery I could plug into anytime I needed a charge.

Good friends are like that. They can lift you when you're down, push you when you're tired, and charge you when you're drained. They can be a wonderful influence in your life.

Best of all, if they're headed for success they'll pull you right along with them.

When I was in college I had friends whose greatest ambition was to guess the Wheel of Fortune puzzles before the contestants. At nights and on weekends they did little besides watch TV, go to movies, and maybe—if they were feeling wild and crazy—order out for pizza.

Hanging out with them, I felt myself turning into a first-class couch potato.

But then I found a new group of friends. People who loved excitement. People who attacked life with zest and energy.

And suddenly my life changed.

At nights we went to dances and parties. On weekends we went boating, skiing, or rappelling. Because of my friends I did more than spend my time watching TV. I learned technical rock climbing. I learned to fly airplanes. I learned to scuba dive.

I learned to *live*.

My friends were such a good influence that my school work improved, too. My best friend was a straight-A student in engineering. I saw how hard he worked for good grades, and I wanted to do the same thing. He was such an influence on me, in fact, that because of him I earned a degree in mathematics.

You might have friends like that yourself. If so, hang on to them. Value them. Appreciate them. They can be one of the best influences in your life.

And if you don't have great friends, make it a goal. Look for people you'd like to be friends with, then get to know them.

I know a young woman named Marsha whose father was an Air Force major. She moved so often that learning to make friends wasn't just nice. It was a matter of survival.

"When you're the new person in school you can't wait for people to come to you," she told me. "If you don't learn to make the first move, you never get to know anyone."

So in class she'd strike up conversations with everyone around her. At lunch, she'd find a table where everyone seemed to be having fun and say: "Hi! Can I sit here?" In the halls, she smiled and said hi to everyone she passed.

Before she knew it, she'd have as many friends as people who had lived there for years.

You need to do the same thing. If you want friends, don't wait for them to come to you. Look for people you'd like to be friends with. Then get to know them. Talk to them. Say hi in the halls. Sit by them in class.

It may seem awkward at first. But if you go out with the attitude that you're going to be friends with someone, before you know it you probably will be.

And be happy! If you're full of gloom and doom—always whining about this and that—people will avoid you like the plague. But if you're upbeat, optimistic, energetic, and happy you'll draw people like a magnet. They'll enjoy your company because you'll make them feel good. You'll help to recharge their batteries.

Think about it. Who would *you* rather spend time with? Someone who moans and groans about every little thing that's wrong in her life? Or someone who makes you laugh and feel good?

People like to laugh. And they like to be happy. So be the bright spot in the life of others.

Another hint is to be genuinely interested in your friends. When they talk, listen. Don't just smile and nod your head once in a while, but really pay attention to what they're saying.

More than that, encourage your friends to talk. Remember that people like to talk about themselves. They like to share things they've done, jokes they've heard, and experiences they've had. When they learn that you're ready with an anxious ear, they'll want to talk with you again and again.

Finally, make them feel important. My friend Melissa was great at this. Whenever she planned an activity, she always made me believe that my presence was the only difference between success and failure.

"I can't believe you can't go!" she wailed once when she organized a ski trip on a weekend when I had other plans. "It's not going to be any fun."

"Melissa, you've got half the school going," I pointed out.

"I know," she said sweetly. "But that's just because everyone thinks you're going to be there."

I knew that wasn't really true. But it made me feel good anyway.

I also remember once talking on the phone to a young man named Jeff. He was telling me how his science teacher surprised the class with a test one day, and how he wasn't ready for it.

"So I started praying to Heavenly Father," he said. "I told Him I didn't have time to study and that I needed all the help I could get."

"And did it work?" I asked.

"Yes! There weren't enough copies of the test, so we didn't have to take it after all."

It was a silly story, but it reminded me that I hadn't been praying as much as I should have. I was impressed that Jeff would pray for help with his school work, and I decided I needed to follow his example.

A week or so later we were talking again, and Jeff told me that he admired me.

"Thanks," I said. "But you know something? I admire you, too."

Jeff couldn't believe it.

"Really? *Why?*"

"Because you're so close to Heavenly Father. After you told me your story about praying last week, I realized I had to pray a little more often, too. And I have been. You were a good influence on me."

"Wow!" he said. "That's cool! You just made my whole day."

That's the way good friends should be—inspiring and motivating one another. Supporting one another. Building one another up. Helping each other to succeed.

So find friends who are zipping toward success and hold on to them. Let them pull you along.

You'll reach success, all right. And the trip will be a blast.

How to Get Started

- Think of someone you'd like to be friends with. Then get to know them! Say hi in the halls. Talk to them in class. Sit by them in lunch. Don't wait for them to make the first move.

- Be positive and upbeat around your friends. Be the spark that keeps their lives energized.

- Listen when your friends talk. Be genuinely interested in what they have to say.

- Find ways to make your friends feel important. Make sure they know that they're important to you.

- Appreciate the good things your friends do for you. Don't take your friends for granted.

11

THERE'S A CANDY BAR IN MY GYM SHOE

The Law of Charity

Here, boy. C'mere, boy."
I held out a piece of hamburger and whistled.
"Come on, boy. Don't be scared, now."

The mangy springer spaniel lay flat against the ground. His ears twitched cautiously, but his tail wagged furiously in the dust.

I moved a step closer. "It's okay, boy. There you go. Sit still, now." I took another step.

The dog cringed, wrinkling his nose as if he expected me to hit him. I held the hamburger a little closer.

"It's okay, boy. I'm not gonna hurt you."

The dog cowered a moment longer, then lifted his head and gingerly took the hamburger. He swallowed the whole thing in two bites.

I reached down and scratched him behind his ears.

I was working at Boy Scout camp when I first saw the stray dog. He wandered into camp once or twice a week, scrounging scraps of food from around the campsites. He was so timid that he ran off whenever anyone came close. And he was so skinny that his ribs showed through his sides.

I felt so sorry for him that I had started sneaking food for him out of the camp kitchen. But this was the first time he had actually let me touch him.

He was in bad shape. I pulled out my pocket knife and sliced off mats of burrs that hung knotted in his fur. I cleaned out his ears and brushed his coat, then got a hose and gave him a good shampoo.

The poor thing was starved for attention. I took him to the rifle range where I worked, and he instantly became the center of attention. Every boy who came up took time to scratch his ears. During classes, Scouts took turns rubbing his belly. At night, he slept in the door of my tent.

In a matter of weeks, Trigger (what else are you going to name a rifle range mascot?) went from a timid, shaggy stray to a friendly, beautiful animal.

But one day I was getting ready for class when I noticed something. As the boys were fussing over Trigger— playing a rowdy game of keepaway—I saw a boy sitting by himself on the bench. I could tell he was lonely. And I suddenly realized there were people who felt just as lost and abandoned as Trigger had.

Everyone in camp went out of their way to give Trigger the love and attention he needed. But all the time we were fussing over Trigger, we were ignoring people who needed our attention just as badly.

In this book we've talked about ways to build yourself up. Ways to help *you* get ahead in life. But there's nothing that will make you feel like a hero as much as helping someone else.

I went to the Post Office one afternoon in December. An elderly man there was trying to mail a Christmas package to his grandson, who was a missionary in England. But he didn't have enough money to send it airmail.

"How long will it take to go by boat?" he asked.

The clerk shrugged. "A month . . . maybe six weeks."

The old man's shoulders slumped. It wouldn't get there in time for Christmas.

Just then, a clerk at the opposite end of the counter called, "Next!"

I stepped up to the window.

"What can I do for you?" he asked.

"I've got a couple of things to send," I said. "But I need you to do me a favor first."

"Sure. What do you need?"

"There's a man at the end of the counter sending a package to England. I'd like to pay for it. And I'd like to send it airmail."

The clerk nodded and started to walk away.

"Just a second," I said. "You can't tell him who's paying for it."

He nodded, then walked down the aisle, where he whispered to the other clerk. When he returned he asked, "Is that your grandfather?"

I shook my head. "No. I've never met him."

"That was nice of you."

I was embarrassed. "It's Christmas," I said.

That particular Christmas I was a little short of money myself. But I felt like a million dollars as I drove home.

At Christmas it's natural to do nice things for people. But you don't have to wait for Christmas. You can do nice things any time you want. You can do it without needing a reason. You can be nice to someone just because they need it.

The exciting thing is that it's not hard to do. You don't have to spend a lot of money. And you don't have to spend a lot of time. You can lift a life with nothing more than a quick note or a cheery smile.

When I was in high school I had a secret friend. I never figured out who she was (I always hoped it was "she"), but she was always leaving notes and candy bars in my locker. Most of them were simple. One said, "Hope you're having a great day," while another one read, "You're the best!"

One time I was having a bad day. But when I opened my locker after lunch, there was a candy bar with a green ribbon tied around it. Underneath was a note: "I hate to see you look so sad. I hope this helps cheer you up."

It worked, too. My secret friend helped me through high school more than she'll ever know.

Take a minute and think about the people around you. Do you know anyone at school who could use a boost? Is there anyone at work who needs a pat on the back? Is there anyone in your neighborhood who could use a friend?

If there is—and you *know* there is!—then here's a chance to be a real hero. Give them the boost! Give them the pat on the back! Be the friend they need!

I was supervising a school dance once when I saw Teresa, a girl from one of my classes. She was standing off to the side, all by herself. She wasn't an attractive girl, and she wasn't very popular. I knew that she wasn't going to dance much.

But I happened to know that she liked a boy named Mike. (She had his name written all over her folders.)

It also happened that Mike was a friend of mine, so I went up to him and said, "How'd you like to do me a favor?"

"Sure."

"There's a girl I'd like you to dance with. Would you ask her?"

76

My respect for Mike went up 100 percent. He didn't ask who she was; he simply said, "Sure."

I pointed her out. And my admiration for him went up another 100 percent. He didn't pull a face. And he didn't say, "Boy, you're gonna owe me big for this one." Instead, he just nodded.

"Okay," he said. "Do you want me to ask her right now?"

I shook my head. "No. Just sometime. I just think it would be cool if she got a chance to dance tonight."

"Okay," he said again. "I'll do it."

He did, too. I saw them as they walked onto the dance floor, and she was *glowing*.

But the classy thing about Mike was that he asked her *twice more*.

Mike lifted a life that night. With no thought for himself—and without worrying what anyone would think—he blessed Teresa's life.

Now, there are kids in your school just like Teresa. Take the time to make them feel important. Make them feel liked. Make them feel needed.

And if you feel embarrassed to do this, remember that no one needs to know. In fact, doing it secretly is sometimes better. Not only can you make someone happy, but you can create a mystery by becoming that person's secret friend. It makes the whole thing more fun.

I have a young friend named Jasen. When he played Little League, he never got much playing time. Even though I thought he was a good batter and fielder, his coach never let him play more than a couple of innings per game.

But Jasen never complained. Even when he was on the bench he'd sit and shout encouragement to his teammates.

I was impressed. I wanted Jasen to know how much I

admired him, but I was embarrassed. So I bought him a batting glove and wrote a note:

> Jasen—
> I like you. I wish I was just like you.
>   a friend

Then I left my present on Jasen's doorstep, rang the doorbell, and ran like mad. I don't know how Jasen felt about it, but it made me feel great.

You'll feel the same way.

So go out of your way to boost the lives of those around you. Put a note in someone's locker. Drop a card in the mail. Leave a present on their doorstep.

And if you really want to have fun, be creative. Hide a candy bar in their gym shoe. Put a note in their math book. Spray a note with perfume.

Sandee, a friend of mine, did this one year at girls camp. She was sitting around the fire with her friends one night when someone mentioned a young woman named Nicole.

"She always looks so sad," someone said.

"I know," someone else agreed. "I don't think I've seen her smile all week."

The unusual thing was that everyone *liked* Nicole. So they decided to let her know it. Secretly.

"We wrote her a note," Sandee said, "and we wrapped it up with a bag of candy. Then we hid it in her sleeping bag."

Sandee said that the fun thing was watching Nicole the next day. Not only did she smile all day, but she kept looking at everyone as if trying to figure out who her "secret friends" were.

"It was so much fun that we did it again," Sandee said. "And then we started doing it for other girls, too. It was the best part of the week."

It's easy to spend all your time worrying about yourself. But when you're sad, lonely, or feeling down, isn't it nice when someone goes out of their way for you?

So do that same thing for someone else. Be aware of the people around you. Lift them when they're down. Boost them when they need it. Be the battery charger that keeps them happy and energetic.

You'll feel great about yourself. You'll have a lot of fun. And you'll know what it's *really* like to be a hero.

How to Get Started

- Think of someone who needs a boost in their life. Then give it to them. Remember that you don't have to wait for special occasions. Give them the boost just because they need it.

- Don't let shyness stop you. If you're embarrassed to reach out to someone, try being a secret friend. Drop a note in their locker. Leave a gift on their doorstep.

- Be creative. Have some fun. Try hiding notes in someone's math book, gym shoe, or lunch bag.

- Keep an eye on your friends, and on family members too. If you appreciate someone, let them know it. If someone's having a bad day, give them a hand up.

12

CRAWLING IN THE ROCKS

The Greatest Discovery of All

The hole in the rock was barely bigger than a basketball. I peered inside for a minute, then snapped off my flashlight and shook my head.

"You really want me to crawl *in* there? You've got to be kidding."

Jack Kelly was grinning like a maniac. Eighteen years old, he was decked out with ropes and carabiners, looking like Indiana Jones. He shook his head. "No! It's great! You've got to try it!"

I glanced inside again. It wasn't really even a hole. It was just a narrow crack in the rock. And because it curved, I couldn't see more than a couple of feet inside.

I was running a three-day rock climbing course at a Boy Scout high adventure base. After two days of climbing and rappelling off the cliffs, we were spelunking through a few of the caves that dotted the mountain. They were everywhere. There were so many, in fact, that we found new ones almost every time we looked.

Like this one. The only difference was that this one wasn't even big enough to stand in.

I got chills just looking at it.

But Jack wasn't bothered a bit. He was one of my climbing instructors, and he was always the first one to try something new or scary. Like now. He cinched up his helmet, snapped on his flashlight, and wiggled inside.

I wasn't excited about following him. But it *was* my camp. I had an image to protect. So I cinched up my helmet, took a couple of deep breaths, and crawled in after him.

Right away I discovered that the crack wasn't the scary thing it had seemed to be.

It was worse!

It was so narrow that I had to crawl along with one arm stretched out in front of me, the other tight against my side. Even then the rocks were so close that I kept getting stuck. One time my helmet got wedged in so tight that it was several minutes before I could twist my way free.

It was scary!

The crack twisted through the rock for about thirty yards, finally widening into a narrow chamber. Jack was there waiting for me, grinning like a little kid at a birthday party.

"This is great, isn't it?"

I nodded vigorously. "Yeah . . . it's not too bad."

By now, I was feeling a little more enthusiastic. I squirmed out of the crack and looked around. The chamber was about five feet across and thirty feet high. There was a glow of light at the top.

"Can we get out that way?"

Jack nodded. "Yeah. Follow me."

He quickly scaled the rock and disappeared. Not being

as agile as Jack, I took a little longer to work my way out. But finally I was wiggling back into the sunshine.

And I had a whole new attitude.

I felt exhilarated! Crawling through that cave pumped me so full of adrenaline that I wanted to turn around and do it again. It was exciting!

Around our campfire that night, Jack was describing the thrill of discovering new caves when somebody said, "I wish I could have lived a hundred years ago."

"Why?"

"Because there were so many things left to discover. Now there's nothing. Everything important's already been found."

My first reaction was to agree. But then I realized that that's not true. The world is *full* of mysteries and surprises. There are still millions of things left to discover. A cure for AIDS, for instance. Or for cancer. Or even for the common cold.

There are regions of the ocean floor left to be mapped or visited by human beings. There are still mountains left unclimbed and valleys that remain unseen.

There are *lots* of things left to explore and discover.

And one of the greatest mysteries is you, yourself.

Think about it. Do you *really* know who you are? Do you know what your talents are? Do you know your limitations? Do you know what great mission your Heavenly Father sent you here to accomplish?

Finding out can be exciting. It can be adventurous. It can be as thrilling as discovering a new country or being the first person to step foot on a new planet.

When I was in high school I had a friend named Christie who is a good example. She decided in tenth grade that she wasn't just going to survive high school. She was going to experience it. So she tried *everything*. If there was a play, she auditioned. If there was an office, she ran. If there was a team, she tried out. Every time you turned around she was joining a club, entering a contest, or attending a dance.

She didn't succeed at everything she tried, but she discovered something that most people never learn: It's not the result that counts. It's the fact that you tried.

Just as important, she learned that *auditioning is half the fun!*

Besides that, she discovered talents, abilities, and interests that she didn't know she had. She learned that she couldn't do everything as well or as easily as some other students, but she found that she had a knack for music and art. She developed new hobbies and made dozens of new friends.

You need to discover what mysteries lie hidden inside you, too. You may not like Christie's approach, but that's okay! Find your own way of unlocking the storehouse of potential within you. Doing it will energize your life.

So stretch your life, expand your horizons, seek your personal limits. Discover what it's like to have a testimony of the gospel. Learn what it's like to make new friends. Find out what's inside you. Bring out the greatness you have hidden inside.

Are you wondering how to do this?

It's easy. Try a new hobby. Make new friends. Try a new sport. Try *anything.*

In fact, if you want to have some fun, go out and try something you think is utterly ridiculous. *Bowling*, for instance.

I used to think bowling was the silliest sport ever invented. I even used to make fun of bowlers ("Yeah, I'm an athlete . . . Number Nine . . . See? I've got my number right here on the back of my shoes . . .").

But over Christmas vacation one year I went bowling with a bunch of friends. And we had a blast! After a couple of games we got goofy and began bowling left-handed. It was one of the best times I've ever had.

After you've done something ridiculous, try something scary. Not dangerous, just *scary*. Like calling a cheer-leader for a date. Or applying for a job. Or trying out for a team.

Find out what it's like to live!

You'll never know what's inside you unless you make the effort to find out.

So do it! Embark now on a journey of self-discovery. Find out what's inside you. Peel away your doubts and limitations. Seek out your true, innermost self.

As you do, you'll have more fun than you can possibly imagine. You'll accomplish things you thought were im-possible. And you'll really become the hero of your own life story.

How to Get Started

- Decide now that you'll never again settle for being anything less than your best.

- Start now and discover what mysteries are hidden within you. Learn what your talents and abilities are. Remember that you'll never know unless you make the effort to find out.

ABOUT THE AUTHOR

Shane Barker is a schoolteacher and freelance writer specializing in sports and outdoor subjects. He has guided white-water trips through the Grand Canyon, cross-country ski treks through the mountains of Utah, and backpacking expeditions through the high country of New Mexico. A former professional scouter, he has served on the faculty of the National Camping School and has conducted courses in outdoor leadership, wilderness survival, and rock climbing. He has written many newspaper and magazine articles, and he is the author of four previous books: *Surviving as a Teenager in a Grown-up's World, Youth Leading Youth, Finding a Friend in the Mirror,* and *Firecracker.*

A graduate of Brigham Young University, he served a mission to Japan for The Church of Jesus Christ of Latter-day Saints. He resides in Orem, Utah.